Mr. Altair's

Simple Guide

To A Complicated

Universe

Mr. Altair's Simple Guide to a Complicated Universe

By Octaevius Altair

ISBN 978-1-312-51405-8

Table of Contents

Introduction

Greetings and welcome to Mr. Altair's Simple Guide To A Complicated Universe. The information contained within this book is derived from the Source Field. It is up to the readers to decide for themselves if they wish to believe or disbelieve any or all of the information contained within this guide. It is not the responsibility of the author to provide proof; only to present the information. This guide will provide a direction for the readers in regards to their personal studies and will cover a wide range of topics such as what the Universe is composed of, how it is designed and how it functions. Unlike a pure scientific approach, we will be melding together physics, thought and spirituality as all these things must combine to create this Living Universe we share.

Space

In truth, it is incorrect to believe that our Universe is divided according to Space. In fact everything shares the same Space. Our Universe is incredibly, highly populated with all forms of life, so dividing it through density of frequency enables many entities to occupy the same space. Space is divided according to density and the Celestial Realms begin at 5th density Space. All space below the 5th density are the realms of Duality, whereas the Celestial Realms of 5th and above are non-duality. Time also exists solely from the 4th density Space and below to prevent the instant manifestation of thought-form. Within the Celestial Realms we will learn the mastery of our consciousness, as it is possible to overcome our Egos and become other things such as Planets, Universes and even assume the Creator consciousness. Within the lower realms (behind the Veil) our task is the mastery of thought-form. No Imperfect thought-form (an addictive thought-form) is permitted within the Celestial Realms. There is only one consciousness and it is the Creator Consciousness of which every Soul is a tiny fraction of and has its own Ego, which is a unique frequency that can be tracked in the Celestial Realms.

All physical constructs that are manifested within the lower realms of 4th density space and below are composed of matter/anti-matter. Those who are familiar with String Theory are aware that the strings that vibrate at a particular frequency determine this expression of matter/anti-matter within these physical realms of duality. These strings themselves are composed of photons –pure light- which must be regarded as the "Body of the Creator". The entire Universe is held together by another energy (some refer to this as "Dark Matter"), which is actually the emotional energy of the Creator (unconditional love). Emotional energy is one of the most powerful energies in existence within our Universe.

Realms of Our Living Universe

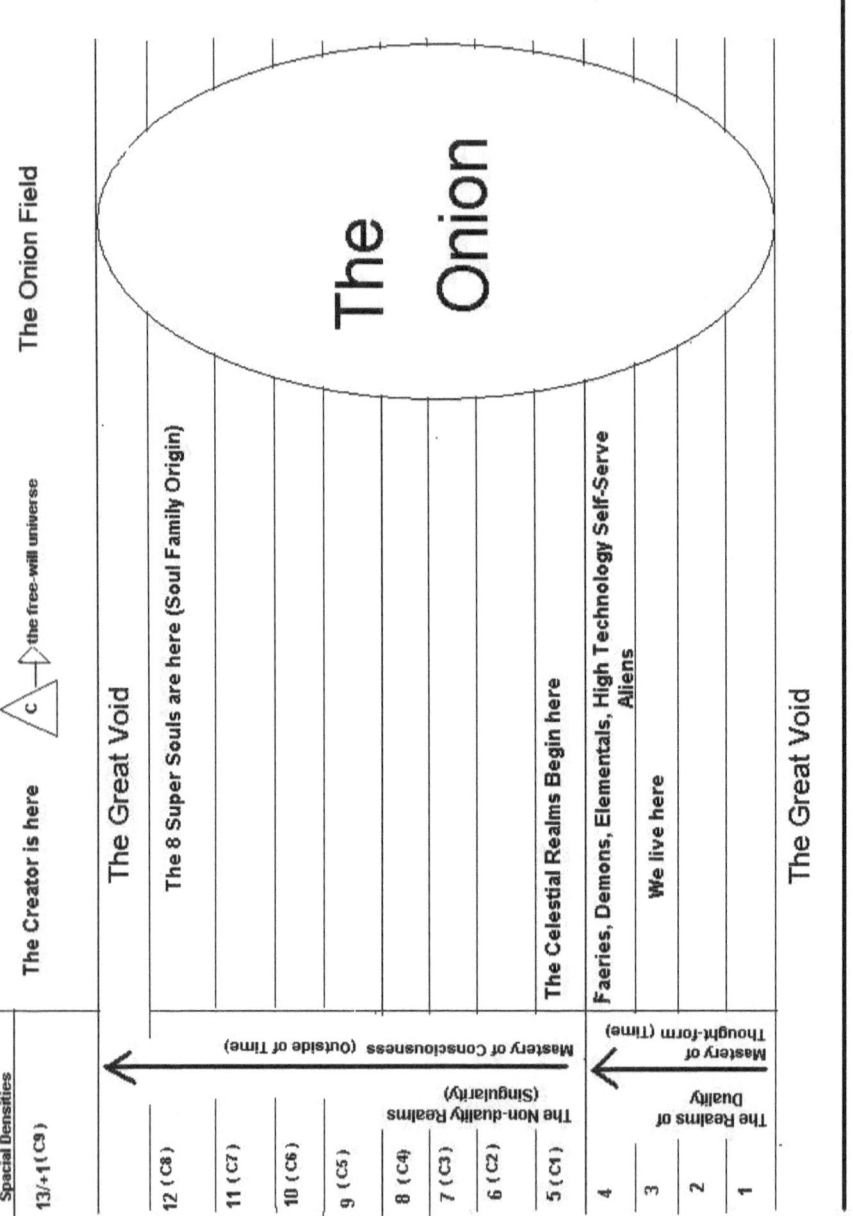

The Onion Field

The Onion

The Creator is here

The Great Void

c ← the free-will universe

The 8 Super Souls are here (Soul Family Origin)

The Celestial Realms Begin here

Faeries, Demons, Elementals, High Technology Self-Serve Aliens

We live here

The Great Void

Mastery of Consciousness (Outside of Time)

Mastery of Thought-form (Time)

The Non-duality Realms (Singularity)

The Realms of Duality

Spacial Densities

13/+1 (C9)

12 (C8)

11 (C7)

10 (C6)

9 (C5)

8 (C4)

7 (C3)

6 (C2)

5 (C1)

4

3

2

1

The Diagram of The Living Universe

To explain the diagram of the Universe it is possible to also compare this to an Onion. It is a single life-form that is composed of multiple layers, yet these layers are not entities unto themselves, just parts of a greater whole. We will use an Onion that has 13 layers. We reside on the 3rd layer and are part of the other layers even though we might not be aware of the activities that occur there on the other layers. Still we are part of a single organism. If we were able to elevate our consciousness to the 13th layer, we would be able to see the Onion Field and recognize that there are other Onions there besides our own. This Universe is a living entity, all stars, planets and living things are part of a single consciousness (Creator Consciousness). Each Soul is a tiny fragment of Creator Consciousness and it is the Ego within each Soul that enables a sense of separateness.

Black Holes and White Holes

In our Universe a balance is maintained in all things, not just between the Light and the Dark but also between the Matter and Anti-matter Universes. It is possible to observe Black Holes in many parts of the Matter Universe. These are actually anti-matter conversion constructs. All matter that is sucked into a Black Hole is converted into anti-matter and expelled out the other end as a White Hole in the Anti-matter Universe. Conversely there are equal expressions within the Anti-matter Universe that suck in anti-matter and then convert and expel this material as matter in our Matter Universe. These constructs again exist in order to maintain balance between these 2 Universes that co-exist next to each other in harmony.

To Comprehend Dimensions

It must be noted that when one examines the juxtaposition of Dimensions –they are generally at 90 degree angles from each other-. This is also mirrored in the Chakras that are also 90 degrees in separation from each other –there are also 12 Chakras-. When we speak of the quality of frequency we understand that the Harmonic Scale consists of 12 notes with the 13th note being the beginning of the next set. So to attempt to imagine that dimensions are of a scale that somehow relates to shape as in a length with a width with an altitude and a time point would be inaccurate. It is more accurate to imagine the shifting upwards in terms of a scale of harmonics in frequency as in wavelengths. It is believed that the wavelength of our present dimension is 7.23. This is the sound of OHM, the average length of the distance between the eyes, the tip of the chin to the tip of the nose and the width of the palm. The shorter the wavelength means the higher the dimension and the longer the wavelength means the lower the dimension. To imagine these as octaves within the musical scale would be to confer that there are 12 Major dimensions and 132 minor dimensions within each Octave (144) – which is not limited in scale as these Octaves go forever in each direction-. Remember also that thought shapes your perception as well as your actual reality.

Excerpt from the book: "33 Steps: from Conception to Ascension Returning to the Source Via the Unorganized Path of Light"

The Heisenberg Uncertainty Principle indicates that through the act of observation at the quantum level, we cause an effect. This could be due to the apparatus used to observe, as any photon will affect the particle. Another method of affect could be the very intent of observation by the observer. Could the intent of the viewer have an affect at the quantum level providing proof of thought-form affecting reality?

Wavelengths

Imagine a beautiful white light passing through a prism. You know that this will cause that light to separate into the base elements of the whole. We are not organic beings but in actuality we are immortal beings of pure light and love. Our souls use this rotting organic matter –flesh- as an avatar through which to gain experience and knowledge here in these lower realms of duality. This is in essence what the term "Duality" means (the separation of the whole). This is where we reside right now. Know that within the colour spectrum we are able to discern only certain wavelengths of colour. Red is the lower and longer wavelength whereas Violet is the higher and shorter wavelength. This is what we discern at present within this "Octave" of our current frequency. Just as colour is a wavelength, so too are our thoughts another wavelength and our emotions yet another. As has been discussed previously, our entire universe is basically just a form of energy wavelength. If we were able to discern both the higher "Octave" as well as the lower; then we would discover that there are yet many more colours of both a longer wavelength than Red and a shorter wavelength than Violet. So too is it with the population of this Universe. We are surrounded by many entities of different wavelengths that we merely cannot perceive. So understand that this reality is indeed composed partially of your very own thoughts and emotions; furthermore that these things effect not only us in our visible universe but also those entities we do not personally perceive.

Excerpt from the book*: "33 Steps: from Conception to Ascension Returning to the Source Via the Unorganized Path of Light"*

Fractal-grid Thinking

Imagine that the known Universe within our present 3rd density space is 13.4 billion light years across. Accept that the speed limit within our Universe is C = 186400.00 miles per second (approx. Speed of Light). This means that in order to transmit a message from one side of our living Universe to the other, would take approx 13 billion years -not very practical-. This is why it is imperative to escape these physical restrictions imposed by the concept of our limited 3rd density spatial paradigms within the physical Universe and accept that our living Universe extends far beyond that. Field-aligned Currents (Birkeland Currents) are a means to transmit signals outside of space-time as these are attracted to Gravitons which are not confined to any particular space-density. It is this attraction to Gravitons that explains why it is that these currents extend from Star to Star throughout the Universe like a vast web, connecting all Stars to each other and from these to all Planets. So the current holds the information while Gravitons carry it to all areas of intended transmission instantly. It is already possible to transmit High definition television signals through these currents (kept classified), so that we could watch a program simultaneously with another being 13 billion light years away. Alpha waves also travel outside our time-space which is why it is possible to receive telepathic messages from any point in the Universe instantly. So the size of our Universe does not pose any difficulty in communication when we transmit outside the barriers of our space density.

Image from
http://en.wikipedia.org/wiki/Birkeland_current

The Currents originate from our Sun (SOL)

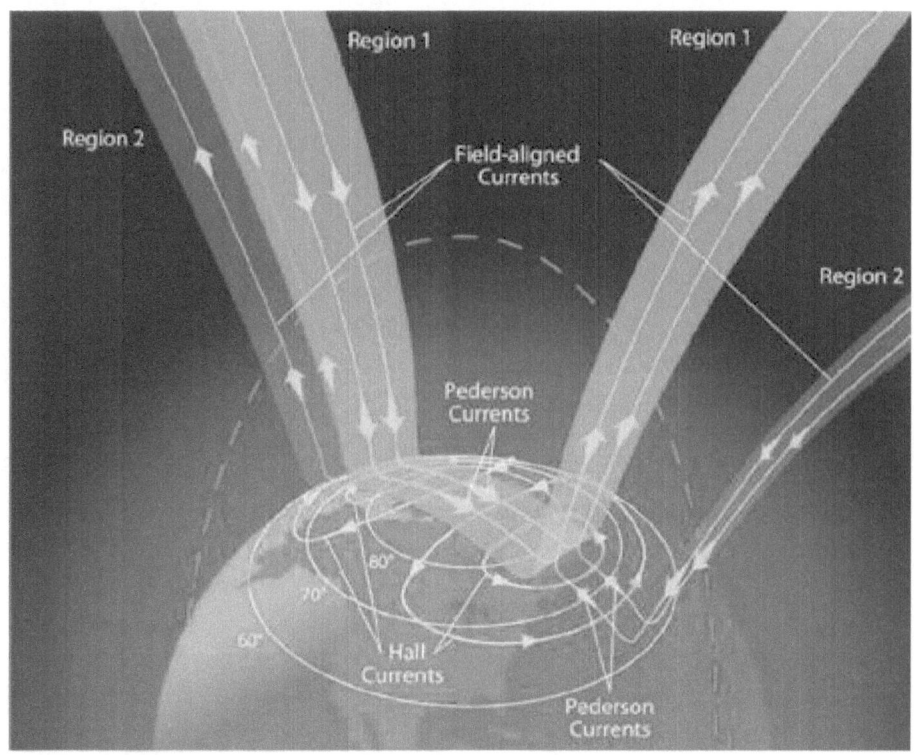

Some definitions of terms used in **Planetary Grid Theory** will be provided below, taken as listed on the **website**
http://www.biogeometry.org/page34.html

Curry lines are a global grid network of electrically charged lines of natural origin. These lines run diagonally to the poles (true or magnetic?) and were first discovered by Dr. Manfred Curry and Dr. Wittmann. There is some disagreement between authorities as to how wide apart these lines are, but the consensus seems to be approximately 3 meters, although most experts recognize that this can vary. The lines themselves are not seen as a problem, only the points where they cross, and obviously lines which run in this way will have numerous intersecting points. As the lines are electrically charged, the intersecting points are double positives, double negatives or one of each. From his studies Dr. Curry felt that the positively charged spots lead to a proliferation of cells, with the possibility of cancerous cell growth, whereas the negatively charged spots could lead to inflammation.

The Hartmann Net (Hartmann Lines) consists of naturally occurring charged lines, running North-South and East-West. It is named after Dr. Ernst Hartmann, a well regarded German medical doctor, who first described it soon after the Second World War. Alternate lines are usually positively and negatively charged, so where the lines intersect it is possible to have double positive charges and double negative charges, or one positive and one negative charge. It is the intersections that are seen to be a source of potential problems.

The Hartmann Net appears as a structure of radiations rising vertically from the ground like invisible, radioactive walls, each 21 centimeters (9 inches) wide. The grid is magnetically orientated, from North to South they are encountered at intervals of 2 meters (6 feet 6 inches), while from East to West they are 2.5 meters (8 feet) apart. Between these geometric lines lies a neutral zone, an unperturbed micro-climate. This network penetrates everywhere, whether over open ground or through dwellings. The points formed by the intersection of these lines, whether positive or negative, are dynamic environments sensitive to the rhythms of the hours and the seasons.

Schumann waves are naturally occurring, beneficial electromagnetic waves that oscillate between the Earth and certain layers of the atmosphere. They were first identified in 1952 by Professor W.O. Schumann, a German scientist. He found that these waves have similar almost the same frequency as brain waves and follow a similar daily pattern. It has been suggested that these waves help regulate the body's internal clock, thus affecting sleep patterns, hormonal secretions, the menstrual cycle in women and so on. The American space agency NASA became interested in this phenomenon when the early astronauts returned to Earth only after a short time in space feeling distressed and disorientated. Subsequently NASA installed equipment to generate Schumann waves artificially in their spacecraft. Some modern buildings with reinforced concrete and metal roofs can inadvertently shield occupants from these beneficial waves. Part of the reason why people suffer from jet lag is that Schumann waves are much weaker at normal airplane altitudes, and this effect is further weakened by the metal fuselage.

Black lines (or deadly energy lines of Chinese Feng-Shui) seem to be naturally generated, although quite how is not known. They may be localized and do not form a network in the same way as Hartmann and Curry Lines. They can be curved, straight, at ground level or higher, even found in the upper levels of buildings. There have been described 2 types of Black lines, one as "black and depressed", the other as "shiny, black, hard and sharp." They could possibly represent the flow lines of a negative type of "orgone-type" energy as described by Wilhelm Reich.

Ley Lines are generally recognized as man-made phenomena, occurring where "sacred stones", which have somehow been charged energetically, are laid in a straight line. The lines appear "naturally" and spontaneously if at least 5 such stones are placed in line within a distance of 25 miles. The stones can be large or small, and the method of charging is thought to be activities such as heating, or impacting with considerable force against other rocks. Other methods could also include ritual washing with spring water, or vibration through the influence of sound.

Planetary Energetic Grid Image from the website
http://www.crystalinks.com/grids.html

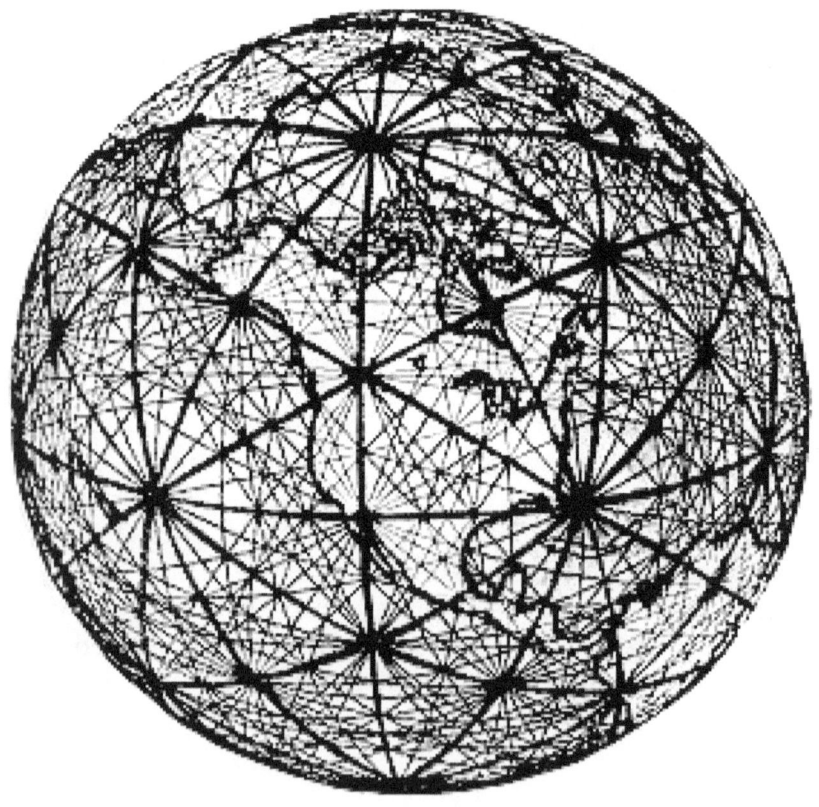

Becker-Hagens Grid: Bill Becker and Bethe Hagens discussed the code of the Platonic Solids' positions on Earth, ascribing this discovery to the work of Ivan P. Sanderson, who was the first to make a case for the structure of the icosahedrons at work in the Earth. He did this by locating what he referred to as Vile Vortices; refer to a claim that there are twelve geometrically distributed geographic areas that are alleged to have the same mysterious qualities popularly associated with the Bermuda Triangle, the Devil's Sea near Japan, the South Atlantic Anomaly and the Marysburgh Vortex of Lake Ontario. Becker and Hagens' attention was drawn to this research through the work of Chris Bird, who published "Planetary Grid" in the New Age Journal in May 1975. After meeting with Bird, they completed their Grid making it compatible with all the Platonic Solids, by inserting a creation from Buckminster Fuller's work.

They proposed that the planetary grid map outlined by the Russian team Goncharov, Morozov and Makarov is essentially correct, with its overall organization anchored to the north and south axial poles and the Great Pyramid at Gizeh. They believed the Russian map lacked completeness, which led them to overlaying a complex, icosahedra-derived, spherical polyhedron developed by R. Buckminster Fuller.

Image from http://www.crystalinks.com/grids.html

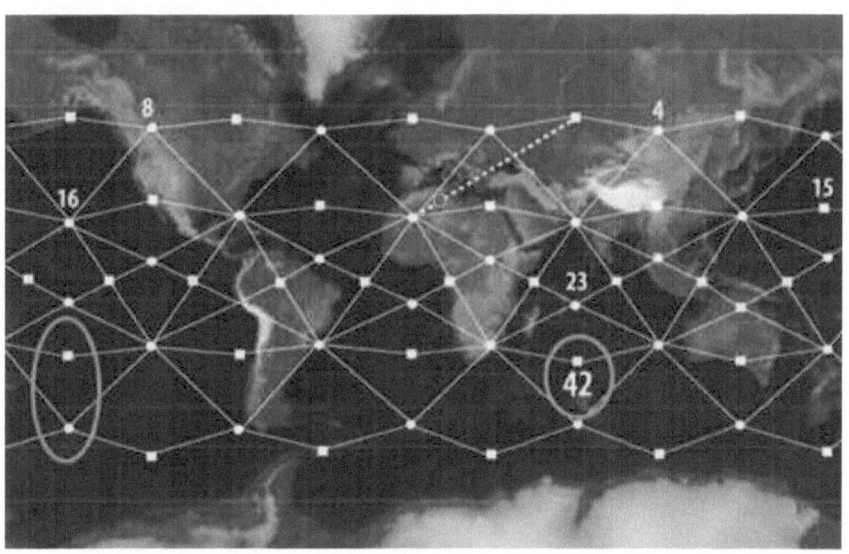

Time and Thought-Form

The residents of this Third Dimensional Realm of Duality (Third Density) are subjects of Time. It is popular to think on this Planet of Time as being somehow linear. Nothing could be further from the truth. There is no such thing as a "Time-line", there are only points in time. This means that whatever experiences you have had in the past will always remain in the past and have no affect whatsoever on your present unless you permit them. There are many on this Planet that seek to dwell not in the present –the only place where you truly exist is the "Now Moment"- but choose to cling to events of their past. Some cling to greatness that they perceive they once had or some others to injustices they suspect that they suffer from. Still this is not healthy because in reality it must be accepted that the only place where we dwell is the present. Those who prefer to dwell in the past will suffer from melancholia (depression) and those who worry about their future will suffer from stress. It is our actions and attitudes that create the future. We are meant to dwell in the present "now moment". It is this creation of individual futures that we each create that manifest in a Pool that may be perceived as the "Collective", that greater future that is shared by all Humanity.

We shall discuss Thought-forms. There are 2 types of these.

Perfect Thought-form is the positive –Light-intents.
Examples: unconditional love, compassion, empathy, mercy, forgiveness

Imperfect Thought-form is the negative –Dark- intents.
Examples: jealousy, pride, anger, hate, vengefulness, selfishness
(Imperfect Thought-form is addictive.)

So here in the moment is the only point in time where we exist at present: furthermore we manifest our future each individual and also as a mass consciousness (Collective). It is important to realize this and to manifest only the Perfect Thought-form manifestation paths into our future and eventual present lives here in the Third Dimension. Unlike the Fifth Dimension where reality is made manifest instantly as this dimension exists outside of time: the Third Dimension is subject to these laws that prevent instant manifestation and only permit direction. It is ultimately each individual that creates His or Her personal future reality based upon the direction of Positive verses Negative Thought-forms. Therefore those who make manifest mostly Positive will have positive things fall in their direction while those who are mostly Negative in Thought-form will have negative experiences made manifest through their direction. It is ultimately reflected upon the Mass-Consciousness of the Collective in a similar manner. More in one or the other direction will produce greater mass positive or negative experiences.

The information I have is from the Source Field. All thoughts stem from the Source Field as it is not possible for the Human Brain to generate even a single thought. The brain serves only to preserve the avatar of flesh (body) your Soul requires to be present here in 3rd Density Space. As all thought exists fully-formed within the Source Field, so it is with D.N.A. All Planets that are capable of supporting Life within 4th Density Space and below will see the D.N.A. manifest from the Source Field. Scientists will say that Evolution is responsible for that and that the Brain is responsible for thought and consciousness (you know this is false). Evolution serves only as a modifier to aid in diversity amongst a species but all D.N.A. exists as do all thoughts within the Source Field. This is why you will discover many of the same plants and animals we have on Earth living on many other Planets throughout the Universe.

The Fetal Development and Energy

In all fetal development it is always the Heart that appears first. This is why the heartbeat is the first thing to occur in all births. From the heart grows the brain next, followed by the rest of the body. So we must assume that the Creator Consciousness that is said to reside within the Heart Chakra of all living things is the first indication of life. With regards to a Human Fetus, the brain grows from the heart and the pineal gland which is said to be the "Cradle of the Soul", is developed by the 49th day. So by day 49, the Human Fetus has both the Creator Consciousness as well as a unique, individual Soul (Ego).

Each type of energy within every human should be perceived as a body. There is the Emotional Body (emotion is a powerful energy), the Mental Body (mental state/thoughts is energy), the Physical Body (physical energy) and finally the Spiritual Body (spiritual energy). There is a theory that certain magnetic fields can result in one of these bodies to go out of sync which then can result in a condition known as sleep paralysis.

Each Human heart has a toroidal field which extends out about 60 ft from the heart and interacts with the other fields of fellow Human beings and their environment. These also interact with the Hartmann Lines found across the surface of the Earth that extend approx 600 ft below the surface. So in this sense, it is apparent that each Human is connected to the Planet and to each other as a result of these interactive energy fields.

Toroidal and Poloidal

Image from Wikipedia, the free encyclopedia
http://en.wikipedia.org/wiki/Toroidal_and_poloidal

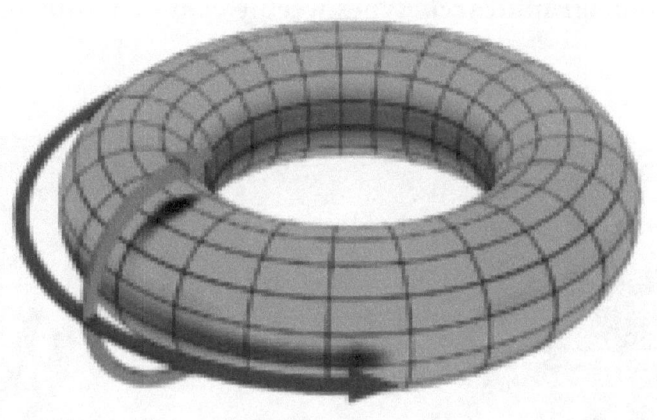

A diagram depicting the poloidal (θ) direction, represented by the red arrow, and the toroidal (ζ or ϕ) direction, represented by the blue arrow.

The Heart Toroidal Field

Image from the website
http://holographicarchetypes.weebly.com/metaphorms-jcer.html

Economic Drivers of Civilization

Below we will discuss the difference between the economic drivers of a Civilization Level One economy and a Civilization Level Zero economy. We will refer to the Level One Civilization as **WORLD ONE** and the Civilization Level Zero as **WORLD ZERO**.

In **WORLD ONE** we will have an economy without any form of currency so the economic drivers are Productivity and Quality. When manufacturing any item in this society it is imperative that all products are built to last and satisfy a need as permanently as possible.

In **WORLD ZERO** we will have an economy based upon the use of currency (worthless small strips of paper covered in cartoons) so the economic driver is Profit. When manufacturing any item in this society it is imperative that all products are built to be temporary so that they will require consistent replacement. The citizens are regarded as consumers whose needs must be placated but never permanently satisfied.

Let's examine some case scenarios.

In **WORLD ONE** a light-bulb is manufactured with the goal of it lasting as long as possible, even hundreds of years. When there is no longer a need to manufacture this item, the Human labour will be diverted to the manufacture of something else. Products here are meant to last and thus all waste is minimized. As all ideas originate in the Source Field, inventions are meant to enrich the entire Human Collective and are property of the Collective.

In **WORLD ZERO** a light-bulb is manufactured with inherent flaws that will render the product useless after a set time and therefore a constant need of manufacture is required and vast waste is generated as a result of this senseless process. Human labour is wasted. Here all inventions are property of the individual and meant to generate paper covered in cartoons for that individual.

———————————————————————————

In **WORLD ONE** a medication to treat a life-threatening disease is manufactured with the intent of permanently ridding the Human Collective of Earth from this disease. So a factory that manufactures a cure for Leprosy will constantly manufacture and distribute this cure to all affected members of the Human Collective on the Planet until there is no longer a reason for it to be manufactured. The Human labour pool involved will then be used to produce something else.

In **WORLD ZERO** a medication to treat a life-threatening disease is manufactured with the intent of permanently maintaining the disease in order to secure a lasting supply of paper covered in cartoons for the factory involved with the manufacture. Examining the present situation on the Planet Earth will reveal that there are many afflicted with Leprosy here but they are economically depressed and therefore unable to provide enough paper covered in cartoons to satisfy the factory that produces the cure. Those Humans in areas of abundant paper covered in cartoons do not have this disease and therefore will not desire it from the factory. So we witness this disease thrive, infecting and ultimately killing thousands of Humans. The factory does not care that the product is only useful to those who lack the paper covered in cartoons to obtain this cure. As long as they can constantly produce it seems to be their only desire, so they try to convince those on the Planet that do not have the disease to provide the paper covered in cartoons to the factory and then resend this to those who actually need it. They do not care about the disease or those members of the Human Collective dying from it. They only care about paper covered in cartoons. Human lives and labour are again wasted.

In **WORLD ONE** an area of the Planet is in need of potable water and irrigation. The need of this area is assessed and all required Human Labour resources are used to treat the problems of this area. The result is an area suddenly abundant in potable water and new areas of irrigated land to produce for the Human Collective that was previously useless.

In **WORLD ZERO** an area of the Planet is in need of potable water and irrigation. The cost in terms of paper covered in cartoons is assessed by those Humans responsible for the affected area. If it is too great for those Humans to produce the required paper covered in cartoons, then the problem is ignored and left to fester. Loss of productive land and perhaps even the lives of Humans and Animals is the result.

In **WORLD ONE** all members of the Human Collective are citizens of the Planet, free to roam and explore their entire world. As all resources are shared, all members have the ability to utilize their innate talents through education or training as these things are rights. Any member of the Collective will be aided to begin any new enterprise that enables them to serve their fellow Humans. There is no wealth or poverty or privatization of any kind.

In **WORLD ZERO** all members of the Human Collective are imprisoned in internment camps which have varying resources available for the prisoners. They are not permitted to roam and explore their world. All resources are privately owned. Members must produce paper covered in cartoons for all education and training as this is a privilege. Many members of the Collective are forced to labour in misery at tasks which do not please them, thus negatively impacting their quality of service. Here there is extreme wealth alongside extreme poverty.

In **WORLD ONE** there is never any labour dispute or strikes or austerity measures imposed. As there is no form of currency there are no budgets or any form of limit upon the Human Collective.

In **WORLD ZERO** there are constant labour disputes and strikes and bizarre austerity measures imposed upon the Human Collective. The Human Collective is forced to depend upon the mass manufacture of worthless small strips of paper covered in cartoons for all of their needs.

It is possible to witness this absurdity with any product. Within our Universe there is only one thing of value and that is labour. All manner of currency in use on the Planet Earth is worthless as are many other things that are programmed within each Human to be perceived as valuable such as gold and gems. Why is this? The only worth these physical things have is the worth that you select to invent and impose upon them. On their own they are merely physical constructs. Only through labour, be it human, animal or through nature, is it possible to accomplish anything. With labour, anything is possible and without it, nothing is possible. To think in terms of labour as energy would be inaccurate. To make any use of unlimited energy requires labour.

This Universe has many realms that are yet to be revealed to our Human Collective. In the Realms of Light, all Souls may lead lives of Bliss where all resources are shared and the Labour of Humans, Animals and Nature are the only things of value. All Souls within this Realm desire only to serve others and lead happy lives of ease as a result. In the Realms of Darkness, all Souls will lead lives of struggle where the resources are not shared equally and therefore a constant state of fear and conflict is maintained. *The greater the number of Souls there who serve only themselves is the greater the darkness of the realm.* Our Planet is presently composed of both those who serve others (Light karmic vibration) and those who serve only themselves (Dark karmic vibration).

Within the realms of duality (4th density space and below) everything must be expressed through polarities. So we see matter/anti-matter, male/female, good/evil, young/old, healthy/sick etc. A common misconception is to infer that this is somehow in opposition to the will of the Creator. This is false. Those Souls who opt to follow the service to self route (organized or unorganized path of darkness) will employ the methods of shame, fear and lies to encourage imperfect thought-form. The Souls who opt to follow the service to others route (organized or unorganized path of light) will employ the methods of pride, courage and truth to encourage perfect thought-form.

Both types of Souls are still from the same Soul Families and are of the Light of the Creator, as are all things. In our Free-will Universe the choice will always be respected yet the Creator still resides within the Heart Chakra of all living things both Dark and Light. The Souls who play the role of the villains must still be loved unconditionally as all other things, for they are still teachers. So it is with the animals as well. Here within the duality realms even animal Souls are free to choose between the service to self and the service to others path. A Buddhist proverb clarifies this seemingly at odds state.

In a school there are employed two brothers as teachers. One is the teacher of the Light while the other is the teacher of the Dark. After the first brother has finished with his lessons he hands the class over to the second brother. "Now class, I have taught you all I can for today so I will permit my brother to begin his lessons to test how well you have learned from me."

So it is in truth that both the Light and the Dark are employees of the same school of Duality, here where we are all pupils.

Soon the "Golden Age" will manifest here on Earth and a great sundering will result. Those of the Light will ascend to Realms where only service to other Souls will reside and those of the Dark will descend into Realms where only service to self Souls will reside. These Realms are created by the Souls who inhabit them just as our present situation on Earth is a construct of our Human Collective here.

As the mythological being Lucifer claimed
"Tis better to rule in Hell than to serve in Heaven".

A story from a priest claims
"A Saint travels to Hell and to Heaven. In both places he views the inhabitants about a grand banquet table. The spoons were 6ft long. In Heaven they are sated, as they take great pleasure in feeding each other. In Hell they are starving."

Prison Planet Earth

The Prison Planet Earth

The Planet Earth and everything on it, within it and in orbit about it is the sole property of the entire Human Collective. Each human is a sovereign citizen of Earth, with the right to travel, live or work anyplace on the planet unhindered.

Despite being initially outlawed by the internment camps, entities that are known as Corporations (owned by a small number of individuals) are permitted to exist. These Corporations gradually seize vast amounts of resources and property from the Human Collective (eventually being granted rights as if they were Human).

Private Banks (owned by a small number of individuals) begin the mass-manufacture of paper with cartoons on it (worthless currency).

The Human Collective

The Private banks lend their worthless, cartoon-covered paper to the internment camps, which then proceed to secure it through tax of the prisoners and rely upon it as a driver for their economy (currency slavery).

The Human Collective are interned in numerous internment camps (countries) managed by puppet governments that have no interest in the welfare of the Collective.

The prisoners within the internment camps are forced to labour for currency and distracted from their enslavement through privately owned media and jailor laws that rely upon Human Sexuality, Narcotics, Religion and Greed in order to distract the Human Collective from its enslavement. Shame, fear and lies are used to keep these unnatural manifestations intact.

The only thing of value in the Universe is Labour. The labour of Humans, Animals or Nature is required for everything and nothing is possible without labour. All Internment Camps, Banks and Corporations must be shut down and everything returned to the Human Collective. Only a Planetary Council working in harmony with City-States (groups of like-minded individuals gathered together within communities of service to each other in unconditional love), will free the Human Collective from imprisonment.

No more physical forms of currency must be permitted to exist on earth, the only family is the Human Family.

Universal Law

Throughout our Universe, there are millions of Civilizations of incarnated Souls. Some are more Dark and some are more Light than ours. Amongst the most spiritually advanced Civilizations, there is the acknowledgement and respect of Universal Law.

Universal Law is as follows:

"All intelligent life is entitled to shelter, all forms of education and all expressions of healthcare. The free-will of the individual will take precedent above all things, provided that they do no harm to others or to their environment."

This law is ignored on Earth at present but soon it will be applied and enforced as we achieve Civilization Level One and abandon the primitive, dark behavior of our Civilization Level Zero.

Please visit this webpage http://www.ngcp.wikifoundry.com to learn more.

Conclusion

Our Universe is in truth a series of overlapping energetic grids that connect from the microcosmic Quantum Universe and its set of laws, to our Macrocosmic Universe with its laws and beyond even that. Like a vast interconnected series of webs, in a grand intelligence, like a brain. This Universe is a single Spiritual expression, of which physical manifestation is only a small part. The physical Universal expression is the same throughout the varying spatial densities. Even the Celestial Realms without time, where all Souls co-exist within an "eternal moment" (eternity means having no beginning) is merely a world where each unique soul generates their own physical space in harmony with the Creator which resides within their Heart Chakra. Eventually we will gain an insight into yet a greater spiritual scope, where our Creator is yet a small part of. Together we are on a journey to Source and all mysteries will be revealed. Here is an attempt to present these mysteries in harmony within "Mr. Altair's Simple Guide to a Complicated Universe."

Mr. Altair's

Simple Guide

To A Complicated

Universe

www.ingramcontent.com/pod-product-compliance
Lightning Source LLC
Chambersburg PA
CBHW050354290526
45785CB00006B/2766